Witness to History

The Arab–
Israeli Conflict

Stewart Ross

H www.heinemann.co.uk/library

Visit our website to find out more information about **Heinemann Library** books.

To order:

☎ Phone 44 (0) 1865 888066

📄 Send a fax to 44 (0) 1865 314091

💻 Visit the Heinemann Bookshop at www.heinemann.co.uk/library to browse our catalogue and order online.

First published in Great Britain by Heinemann Library,
Halley Court, Jordan Hill, Oxford
OX2 8EJ, part of Harcourt Education.
Heinemann is a registered trademark of
Harcourt Education Ltd.

© Harcourt Education Ltd 2004
The moral right of the proprietor has been asserted.

Produced for Heinemann by Discovery Books Ltd
Editorial: Nancy Dickmann, Tanvi Rai and
    Kathryn Walker
Design: Rob Norridge and Ron Kamen
Picture Research: Rachel Tisdale
Production: Séverine Ribierre

Originated by Dot Gradations
Printed and bound in China by South China
Printing Company

ISBN 0 431 17057 6
08 07 06 05 04
10 9 8 7 6 5 4 3 2 1

British Library Cataloguing in Publication Data
Ross, Stewart
    The Arab-Israeli Conflict. – (Witness to History)
    956'.04

A full catalogue record for this book is available from
the British Library.

Acknowledgements
The publishers would like to thank the following for
permission to reproduce photographs: Bettmann/Corbis
pp. **7**, **24**, **28**, **30**, **33**; Corbis pp. **5**, **8** (Richard T Nowitz),
10, **20**, **34** (Francoise de Mulder), **36**, **40** (David H
Wells), **45** (Eldad Rafaeli), **47** & **48** (Ricki Rosen), **50**;
Corbis Saba p. **46** (David Bukow); Corbis Sygma pp. **6**
(Halawani Rula), **38** (Maher Attar), **42** (Aubert-Milner);
Hulton-Deutsch Collection/Corbis pp. **14**, **21**; Reuters
NewMedia Inc./Corbis p. **44**; Popperfoto.com pp. **12**,
18, **27**, **35**; Topham Picture Point pp. **13**, **15**, **16**, **22**,
26, **32**, **37**.

Cover photograph of a Palestinian teenager hurling a
stone at an Israeli tank in a refugee camp in the West
Bank, November 2003, reproduced with permission
of Reuters/Abed Omar Qusini.

The publishers would like to thank Bob Rees, historian
and assistant head teacher, for his assistance in the
preparation of this book

Every effort has been made to contact copyright
holders of any material reproduced in this book. Any
omissions will be rectified in subsequent printings if
notice is given to the publishers.

The paper used to print this book comes from
sustainable resources.

Words appearing in the text in bold, **like this**, are explained in the glossary.

Contents

Introduction 4

How do we know? 6

A holy land 8

Conflicting interests 10

Mandate 12

Holocaust 14

Exit Britain, enter the UN 16

Israel, 1948–49 18

Digging in, 1949–55 20

Suez 22

The Palestinians organize 24

The Six-Day War, 1967 26

Resolution 242 28

Arab versus Arab 30

Yom Kippur 32

The conflict spreads 34

Camp David 36

Mounting violence 38

Intifada 40

PLO recognition and isolation 42

Signs of hope, 1991–96 44

Terror and counter-terror 46

The road map 48

What have we learnt? 50

Timeline 52

Find out more 53

Primary sources 53

Glossary 54

Index 56

Introduction

The Arab-Israeli conflict is essentially about land. Two peoples, the Jews and the Arabs, both claim the same territory along the eastern shore of the Mediterranean. The Jews know this land as Israel, the Palestinian Arabs, who also live there, call it Palestine.

Nationalism makes the situation more complicated. This movement, which first appeared in the 18th century, means creating a feeling of togetherness between people living within a country. Often speaking the same language and sharing the same values and way of life, they have a common love of their native land.

Israeli nationalism blossomed as soon as the country was set up in 1948. Palestinian nationalism emerged more slowly because the Palestinian Arabs had never had a country of their own, but by the 1980s it was a powerful force. So the Arab-Israeli conflict became a clash between two nations, as well as a battle over land.

A tangled web

Religion and race make the conflict more bitter still. Some Israelis, unshaking in their Jewish faith, believe they are God's chosen people and He has given the land of Israel to them. Similarly, some Palestinians are devoted Muslims who believe it is their holy duty to drive out the 'unbeliever' Jews. This clash of faiths makes the conflict much harder to solve.

Present-day Israel and its neighbours, showing the **Gaza Strip** and the West Bank.

4

Fighting for water: Israeli tanks seize the fertile Golan Heights in 1967. The area's many streams feed the River Jordan, a key water supply for the entire region.

Intervention by neighbouring Arab countries with little genuine concern for the Palestinians has made the situation yet more complex. Furthermore, for years the conflict was linked to a wider global clash, the **East** versus **West** confrontation known as the **Cold War**.

This worldwide dimension has continued into the 21st century, involving Jews living outside Israel and Arabs outside Palestine. Some Palestinians, allegedly trained outside the region and sponsored by non-Palestinians, have resorted to **terrorist** tactics such as suicide bombings. After the 11 September 2001 terrorist attacks on New York and Washington, the Arab-Israeli problem became entangled with the US-led 'War Against Terrorism'. This drew Palestinian terrorists into the USA's campaign against global terrorism.

A final element in understanding the complexity of the Arab-Israeli conflict is its longevity. By 2003 it had lasted for more than half a century, and the longer it went on, the more difficult it became to settle. Generations had grown up knowing nothing but the struggle, inheriting the prejudices, the horror stories, the **martyrdoms** and the hatreds of their predecessors. Children on both sides were raised and educated in the conflict – it was part of their heritage, something it was their duty not to betray.

How do we know?

There are two types of source about the Arab-Israeli conflict: primary and secondary. **Primary sources** include anything from personal recollections to government documents. **Secondary sources** are books, articles, videos, websites and so forth produced by people who have studied the conflict.

A Jordanian TV crew records the bitter grievances of the Palestinians living in Jericho, 1994.

The number and variety of sources on the Arab-Israeli conflict is vast. As well as printed material, film, video, photographs, letters and so on, every Palestinian Arab and Israeli has their own story to tell. This helps and hinders students seeking to produce an unbiased understanding of events – an account that is not affected by personal opinion.

The number of sources, from peace **treaties** to interviews, makes it quite easy to piece together a basic outline of events. We have, for example, a fairly accurate record of fighting during the Six-Day War of 1967 (see page 26). Historical facts, however, especially about recent events, are usually seen from a particular point of view. A good example is the name of a war that started in 1948 (see page 18): to the Palestinian Arabs it is known simply as the 'Disaster' while in Israel it is the 'War of Independence'. Both are accurate because they describe the same event seen through different eyes.

Where is the truth?

Another difficulty is that the conflict is still going on. We do not know what the eventual outcome will be. Therefore, at this stage it is difficult to distinguish the sources that shed light upon central themes of the conflict from those that deal with issues of lesser, passing importance. Only time, for instance, will enable us to assess rationally the parts played by men like Palestinian leader Yasser Arafat and Israeli prime minister Ariel Sharon.

Language presents further difficulties, as translations rarely capture the precise meaning of the original word or phrase. The Arabic word '**Intifada**', for example, literally means 'shaking off' (see page 40), although to Palestinians it conveys a great deal more because of its association with ideas of uprising, justice and freedom.

Finally, it is almost impossible not to feel some sort of emotional involvement with events in Israel-Palestine, and this is bound to colour one's reaction to what one sees and hears. For some people, a suicide bomber blowing himself or herself up and killing and injuring dozens of civilians (see page 46) may be regarded as cold-blooded **terrorist** murder, for others it might seem a brave and blessed act in the cause of justice and freedom. That difference is at the root of the region's enduring tragedy.

1972 Munich Olympics: TV audiences around the world watch as an official of the International Olympics Committee talks to a hooded member of the Palestinian gang that had invaded the Olympic village. Nine Israeli athletes were killed.

A holy land

The origins of the modern Arab-Israeli conflict reach back beyond history into the realms of legend, perhaps even to the hostility between two of the sons of the Old Testament figure, Abraham. For the purposes of this book, however, we will take up the story in the second half of the 19th century.

At that time most of the Middle East was part of the crumbling Turkish **Ottoman** Empire. The region of modern-day Israel-Palestine was governed as Palestine, a district within the huge Ottoman province of Greater Syria. Palestine was of great religious importance to Jews and Christians. It was the Jews' 'holy land' of the Old Testament, the place where their faith had been born. However, by about AD 100 the bulk of the Jewish inhabitants of the ancient state of Israel had spread throughout Europe and the Middle East – a dispersal known as the 'Diaspora'. Although frequently persecuted, the Jews maintained their faith and traditions.

To Christians, Palestine was the land where Jesus Christ had lived and died. Jerusalem, the district's most important city, was also holy to Muslims. From its Holy Rock the Prophet Mohammed ascended into heaven. The city teemed with the faithful of many beliefs, from American Christian missionaries to Muslim **pilgrims**. The rest of the land was populated largely by Muslim Arabs, who until the 1890s lived in peace with a small number of Jews. Ominously, in June 1891 there occurred the first outbreak of violent Arab-Jewish hostility.

Mosque, church and synagogue – the city of Jerusalem, perhaps the most divided community in the world, is holy to Muslims, Christians and Jews.

Theodor Herzl calls for a Jewish State

In the 1890s, as **nationalism** flourished throughout Europe, Jews were persecuted nearly everywhere. In 1896 an Austrian Jew called Theodor Herzl published a pamphlet entitled *The Jewish State*, in which he suggested that for the Jews, too, the solution would be to have a state of their own.

Oppression and persecution cannot exterminate us [wipe us out]. No nation on earth has survived such struggles and sufferings as we have gone through. Jew-baiting has merely stripped off our weaklings; the strong among us were invariably [always] true to their race when persecution broke out among them. . .

I do not intend to arouse sympathetic emotions on our behalf. That would be a foolish, futile, and undignified proceeding. I shall content myself with putting the following questions . . . Is it not true that, in countries where we live in perceptible numbers, the position of the Jewish lawyers, doctors, technicians, teachers and employees of all descriptions becomes daily more intolerable?. . .

Everything tends, in fact, to one and the same conclusion, which is clearly enunciated in that classic Berlin phrase: '*Juden Raus!*' (Out with the Jews!). . .

I shall now put the [Jewish] Question in the briefest possible form: Are we to 'get out' now and where to?. . .

[My] whole plan is in its essence perfectly simple, as it must necessarily be if it is to come within the comprehension of all.

Let the sovereignty [control] be granted us over a portion of the globe large enough to satisfy the rightful requirements of a nation; the rest we shall manage for ourselves.

Conflicting interests

When war broke out in Europe in 1914, the **Ottoman** Turks allied with Germany, which was fighting Britain, France, Russia and, later, the USA. To hamper their Ottoman enemies, the British encouraged **revolt** within the Ottoman Empire. This meant supporting breakaway **nationalist** movements.

Arab nationalism originated among graduates of the American University of Beirut. It called for self-government for all Arab peoples, who should be free to decide the division of their territories. In 1915 a British diplomat in Cairo, Sir Henry McMahon, won the support of Sharif Hussein, one of the most influential Arab leaders. Together they agreed that the Arabs would join the war against the Ottomans in return for self-government over much of Greater Syria after the war.

Meanwhile, the British government was also eager to get Jewish support, particularly as the movement for the establishment of a Jewish state in Palestine ('**Zionism**') was gathering momentum. Consequently, in November 1917 the foreign secretary Arthur Balfour declared that his government was in favour of a Jewish 'national home' in Palestine.

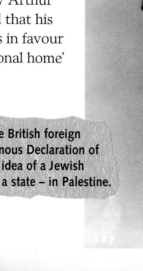

Arthur J. Balfour, the British foreign secretary, whose famous Declaration of 1917 supported the idea of a Jewish homeland – but not a state – in Palestine.

Sir Henry McMahon's letter
In a letter to Sharif Hussein of Mecca dated 24 October 1915, Sir Henry McMahon explains the parts of Palestine in which he will accept Arab self-government. Some people say Hussein believed these regions included the territory later claimed by Zionists.

The two districts of Mersina and Alexandretta and the portions of Syria lying to the west of the districts of Damascus, Homs, Hama and Aleppo cannot be said to be purely Arab, and should be excluded from the limits demanded. . .

As for the regions lying within those frontiers wherein Great Britain is free to act without detriment [harm] to the interests of her ally, France, I am empowered in the name of the Government of Great Britain to give the following assurance and make the following reply to your letter:

(1) Subject to the above modifications, Great Britain is prepared to recognize and support the independence of the Arabs in all regions within the limits demanded by the Sharif [Hussein] of Mecca.

Balfour's letter
In support of their cause the Zionists cited Balfour's Declaration, contained in a letter to the British Zionist leader Lord Rothschild dated 2 November 1917. In some eyes, the British seemed to have promised the same territory to two different peoples.

His Majesty's Government view with favour the establishment in Palestine of a national home [note that the word 'state' is not used] for the Jewish people, and will use their best endeavours to facilitate the achievement of this object [do their best to help them achieve this], it being clearly understood that nothing shall be done which may prejudice the civil and religious rights of existing non-Jewish communities in Palestine, or the rights and political status enjoyed by Jews in any other country.

Mandate

British forces under General Allenby, assisted by Arab irregulars – troops that were not trained under the authority of their government – defeated the Turks and took possession of Palestine in 1918. Then, apparently contrary to its wartime pledges, Britain remained in the region. Its position was confirmed by the **League of Nations** in 1920. Palestine was a British **mandate** – a territory governed by Britain on behalf of the international community.

Although Britain was supposed to prepare Palestine for self-government, the British presence infuriated Jews and Arabs, both of whom felt betrayed. The 1920s and 1930s were marked by three-way (British-Arab-Jewish) dislike and mistrust that sometimes descended into violence. The creation of institutions of self-government met with greater success among the Jews than the Arabs, who were divided by traditional loyalties.

The situation deteriorated further after an Arab–Jewish **massacre** in Jerusalem in 1929. Throughout the land 116 Arabs and 133 Jews died. Seven years later, with Jewish **immigration** to the region soaring, the Arabs launched a full-scale rebellion. Asked by the British government to examine the Palestinian situation, a special **commission** recommended that the land be divided or **partitioned**, between Jews and Arabs. The British Government and the Arabs rejected the idea.

General Allenby, the British general who, with Arab support, broke the power of the Turkish Empire in much of the Middle East during World War I.

The Royal Commission's report

The British Royal Commission under Lord Peel, asked to examine the causes of the 1936 Arab **Revolt** and advise on the future of Palestine, was certain that Jews and Arabs could not live together. Nowadays its proposal for partition of the region into two states seems wise and far-sighted.

An irrepressible conflict has arisen between two national communities within the narrow bounds of one small country. About 1,000,000 Arabs are in strife, open or latent [ready to break out], with some 400,000 Jews. There is no common ground between them. The Arab community is

The trouble begins: violence breaks out between Arabs and the Jewish minority in Jerusalem, May 1920.

predominately Asiatic in character, the Jewish community predominately European. They differ in religion and language. Their cultural and social life, their ways of thought and conduct, are as incompatible as their national aspirations [hopes]. These last are the greatest bar to peace. Arabs and Jews might possibly learn to live and work together in Palestine if they would make the genuine effort to come to reconcile and combine their national ideals and so build up in time a joint or dual nationality. But this they cannot do. The War [World War I] and its sequel have inspired all Arabs with the hope of reviving in a free and united Arab world the traditions of the Arab golden age. The Jews similarly are inspired by their historic past. They mean to show what the Jewish nation can achieve when restored to the land of its birth. National assimilation [joining together] between Arabs and Jews is thus ruled out . . . Neither Arab nor Jew has any sense of service to a single state. . .

13

Holocaust

In the 1920s many European Jews had left their countries to live in America. However, high unemployment in the 1930s, brought about by the worldwide economic downturn known as the **Great Depression**, led the US to stop the **immigration** of Jews. This happened at the same time as the **Nazi** party was persecuting German Jews with great violence. The US action left Palestine as the European Jews' major haven from the anti-Jewish policies of Adolf Hitler. In 1939 the British decided to limit immigration there to 15,000 a year. Although many more were smuggled in, the quota meant that many millions of others had nowhere to go to escape persecution by Nazis.

World War II (1939–45) increased American interest in the Palestinian situation because US politicians wanted the support of American-Jewish business interests in the war effort. As a consequence of the Great Depression, and events during the war, American calls for a Jewish homeland grew louder.

Meanwhile, the British were trying to keep on good terms with the Arab world because of its vital oil reserves. At the same time, because they were at war with Hitler, the British were bound to support the people Hitler hated most, the Jews. By 1945 this balancing act had become too much: Britain had neither the money nor the will to hold on to its troublesome Palestinian **mandate** any longer.

Fleeing persecution in Russia and elsewhere in Eastern Europe, Jewish immigrants flood the wharf in Haifa, Palestine, 1929. Worried that the number of immigrants would lead to increased tension between Jews and Arabs, the British imposed strict limits on Jewish immigration.

Frima Laub recalls hiding from the Nazis after they had invaded the Soviet Union.

In trying to wipe out all European Jews, the Nazis killed perhaps six million people between 1939 and 1945. This slaughter is known as the '**Holocaust**'. After invading the **Soviet Union** in 1941, the Nazis rounded up and killed as many Soviet Jews as they could find. Frima, aged only five in 1941, survived.

My mother . . . left me in [this] lady's house. . . After two weeks the lady . . . was really afraid to keep a Jewish child in the house because . . . the Germans notified everyone that if a Jew was found in their house [it] would be burned and the family would be killed. . . And so she told me I had to leave her house . . . and so I walked out of the house. . . I really needed help and I remembered this lady whom my parents were friendly with. . . And it

The crime that shamed the world: Jewish women in a 'death camp' as part of the Nazi scheme to exterminate their race. This Holocaust made it almost impossible to resist plans for the establishment of a Jewish homeland.

was winter and cold and the snow was maybe five, six inches [deep]. And I made it to her house and as I got to her gate . . . her dog started barking so she came out to see . . . and she sees me and she says, 'My God, come in quick. Come in quick.' And she takes me to her barn because obviously she must have noticed that I had lice crawling all over me . . . She said to me, 'Where are your parents?' I said, 'Everybody is killed. Everybody is dead.' Because I wanted her to have pity on me. And so she did.

Exit Britain, enter the UN

By mid-1947 the situation in Palestine was more complicated than ever. The British were fighting **Zionists** and at the same time handing over control of Palestine to the newly-formed **United Nations** (UN). Zionists believed their time had come. They had backing from the USA, and sympathy from the international community because of the many Jews that died in the **Holocaust**. Arab-Jewish suspicions and violent confrontations continued.

King Abdullah of Transjordan (later simply Jordan), the Arab monarch who seized the lands on the west bank of the River Jordan that the United Nations had earmarked for the Palestinians.

Arab states, which in 1945 had formed the **Arab League**, were openly determined never to see a Jewish state on what they said was Arab land. In secret, however, some of them, such as King Abdullah of **Transjordan** (now Jordan), made agreements with the Zionists to carve up the land of the local Arabs.

The UN set up a committee (the UN Special Committee for Palestine, UNSCOP) to investigate the Palestine situation. It recommended that the land be **partitioned**, with Jerusalem under international control. In November 1947 the UN **General Assembly** accepted this plan by 33 votes to 13. Neither the Israelis nor the Arabs were happy with the frontiers proposed by the UN. As both sides prepared to take matters into their own hands, war seemed almost inevitable.

The Partition Resolution

As only the **Security Council** may agree UN action, the Resolution passed by the UN General Assembly on 29 November 1947 was simply a recommendation. As we can see from its wording, it was perhaps too optimistic and unrealistic.

Resolution on the Future Government of Palestine

The General Assembly,

. . . *Considers* that the present situation in Palestine is one which is likely to impair [harm] the general welfare and friendly relations among nations. . . [and] *Recommends* to the United Kingdom, as the mandatory Power for Palestine, and to all other Members of the United Nations the adoption and implementation [agreeing and carrying out] . . . of the Plan of Partition . . . set out below;

Plan of Partition

Part I – Future Constitution and Government of Palestine

1. The **Mandate** for Palestine shall terminate as soon as possible but in any case not later than 1 August 1948. . .

3. Independent Arab and Jewish States and the Special International regime for the City of Jerusalem . . . shall come into existence in Palestine two months after the evacuation of the armed forces of the mandatory Power has been completed but in any case not later than 1 October 1948. The boundaries of the Arab State, the Jewish State, and the City of Jerusalem shall be as described below. . .

10. ...each state shall draft a **democratic** constitution for its State and chose a provisional [temporary] government. . . The constitutions of the States shall embody [contain] chapters . . . for . . . settling all international disputes in which the State may be involved by peaceful means in such a manner that international peace and security, and justice, are not endangered.

Israel, 1948–49

By the spring of 1948 the Palestine situation was out of control, with Jews and Arabs in open (but undeclared) combat. Following **massacres** on either side in April, on 14 May 1948 the Jewish leadership of President Chaim Weizmann and Prime Minister David Ben Gurion declared that the territory suggested by the **United Nations** had become a new state: Israel. Egypt, Lebanon, **Transjordan**, Syria and Iraq declared war on it the following day. Their aim, they said, was to **liberate** Palestine.

The fighting lasted on and off until early in 1949. After initial setbacks, the better led and more heavily armed Israeli forces won several victories and ended up with a country 21 per cent larger than before. There were Arab gains, too: Transjordan acquired the **West Bank**, and Egypt the **Gaza Strip**.

The biggest losers were the Palestinian Arabs, who now had no immediate hope of establishing their own state. 150,000 Palestinians lived in the expanded Israel, 450,000 in Transjordan, and 200,000 in Egypt. Most tragic of all, perhaps 700,000 of them were **stateless**, homeless **refugees**. The Palestinian-Israeli conflict had begun.

Fighting for survival: Israeli Jeep **commandos** firing as they drive through an Arab-populated village during the war of 1948–49. Neighbouring Arab states had declared their intention of driving the Israelis into the sea and destroying their new state.

Alfred M. Lilienthal's letter

By no means did all Jews welcome the creation of the state of Israel. Some, such as the American Jew Alfred M. Lilienthal, believed being Jewish was a matter of faith, not nationality. He expressed his hostility to **Zionism** in this published letter to his mother.

Dear Mother . . .

Only last year, a new white flag with a single blue six-pointed star was hoisted to a mast many thousands of miles away on the east coast of the Mediterranean Sea. This flag of Israel is the symbol of a new **nationalist** state, with its own government, army, foreign policy, language, national anthem and oath of allegiance.

And this new flag has brought every one of us five million American citizens of the ancient faith of Judah to a parting in the road.

Judaism, I have felt, was a religious faith which knew no national boundaries, to which a loyal citizen of any country could adhere [hold on to]. By contrast, Zionism was and is a nationalist movement organized to reconstitute [re-establish] Jews as a nation with a separate homeland. . .

Let us start, Mother, with how I feel about this new State of Israel. I wish it well. I hope that several hundred thousand suffering displaced persons will find in it a happy home. . . But when its flag was first raised on May 14, 1948, I had no impulse to dance in the street with hysterical joy. . . For I was born and remain an American. . .

The plain fact is that we Jews are not a race and we should not let the Zionists persuade us that we are.

Digging in, 1949–55

There were **cease-fires** after the war of 1948–49, but no Arab state openly admitted the right of Israel to exist. All countries in the region were new creations with comparatively inexperienced governments. No single leader or government was powerful or respected enough to guide towards a general peace. Of the other powers who might have done so, Britain and France were adjusting to their new roles as second-rate powers, and the **Cold War** prevented either the USA or the **Soviet Union** from making a move.

Again, it was the Palestinians who suffered. No one took responsibility for them. The Israelis said Arab **propaganda** had caused the Palestinians to flee; the Arabs said the Israelis had driven them out. Those with money and contacts tried to rebuild their lives in other Arab states. The majority were too poor to do more than stagger over the Israeli border to makeshift accommodation in **refugee** camps in **Gaza**, Lebanon and on the **West Bank** of the River Jordan. Time and again the Arab-Israeli conflict returned to the same sticking point: what should be done about the Palestinian refugees?

The wise man of the Middle East: **Western-**educated King Hussein I on his accession to the throne of Jordan in 1953. He spent much of his reign battling to prevent his poor country from being swallowed up in the Arab-Israeli conflict.

Interview with Mohammed Allawi

Mohammed Allawi's family left Palestine in 1948, fleeing what they believed to be certain death at the hands of the Israelis. Having a little money, they travelled across **Transjordan** and eventually settled in Saudi Arabia.

What can I tell you? Of course I don't like it here. No one does. I want to go home, to Palestine, where I grew up. But I can't. Even if I wanted to go there, they would not let me in. Now we belong nowhere. The Saudis don't like us, they don't want us in their country. Nor do any of the other Arabs. We are a nuisance to them. Do you know what they say we are? They say we're the Jews of the Arab world – the people who wander about, the scroungers, ones who do not belong, who do not fit in.

Palestinian refugees, rendered homeless by the First Arab-Israeli War (1948–49), head for a makeshift camp under **United Nations** supervision.

You cannot imagine what it is like. You have a passport, you have a country which you belong to. You have a place in the world. We do not. I don't even have a passport, just refugee papers. What can I do? I can work hard and get a degree and a maybe, God willing, a good job. But then the Saudis will hate me more because I am taking good money from them. But I know that they could not survive without us to help them. We, the Palestinians, do all the skilled work here – the plumbing, electricity and so on. There is no Arab unity. The Arabs hate each other as much as they hate the Jews.

21

Suez

The Arab-Israeli war of 1948–49 solved nothing. The leading Israeli politician was David Ben Gurion (prime minister 1948–53 and 1955–63). He believed the Arabs would never accept the state of Israel, so he followed a policy of 'aggressive security'. This meant building up the country's armed forces, damaging Arab states where possible and **retaliating** fiercely whenever Israeli citizens were threatened. By the 1950s such retaliations became more frequent in the face of raids by Palestinian **commandos** (the *fedayeen*). These guerrilla fighters were mostly based in Egypt.

Arab hopes rose in 1954 when the dynamic and popular Gamal Abdul Nasser became prime minister of Egypt. He managed to get aid from both the **superpowers**, the **Soviet Union** and the USA, and rearmed his country. He also seized the Suez canal in July 1956, the vital shipping route that passed through Egyptian territory. Britain and France were alarmed by Nasser's action and secretly allied with Israel to remove him from power. The three-power assault in October/November 1956 was a military success but a **diplomatic** disaster. The Soviet Union and the USA refused to support the attack, the Anglo-French troops withdrew and a **UN** force arrived to supervise the **cease-fire**. Nasser became an instant hero – the Arab who had beaten off three major powers at once.

Hail the hero! Wildly cheering Egyptians greet their president, Gamal Abdul Nasser, after he had announced that he had nationalized the Suez Canal.

The Sèvres agreement

In late October 1956, British, French and Israeli commanders held a secret meeting at Sèvres, France, to arrange an attack on Egypt. As this document shows, they hatched a crude excuse for going to war to take back the Suez Canal which Nasser had nationalized – made the property of Egypt – in July.

1. The Israeli forces launch in the evening of 29 October 1956 a large-scale attack on the Egyptian forces with the aim of reaching the [Suez] Canal zone the following day.

2. On being appraised [told] of these events, the British and French governments during the day of 30 October 1956 . . . make two appeals to the Egyptian Government and the Israeli Government on the following lines:

(a) To the Egyptian Government
    (i)   halt all acts of war
    (ii) withdraw all its troops ten miles from the Canal
    (iii) accept temporary occupation of key positions on the Canal by the Anglo-French forces.

(b) To the Israeli Government
    (i)   halt all acts of war
    (ii) withdraw all its troops ten miles to the east of the Canal.

It is agreed that if one of the Governments refused, or did not give its consent, within twelve hours the Anglo-French forces would intervene.

3. In the event that the Egyptian Government should fail to agree within the stipulated time to the conditions of the appeal addressed to it, the Anglo-French forces will launch military operations against the Egyptian forces in the early hours of the morning of 31 October.

6. The arrangements of the present protocol [agreement] must remain strictly secret.

The Palestinians organize

By 1960 the Palestinian leaders understood full well that the Arab states bordering Israel – Egypt, Jordan (formerly **Transjordan**), Syria and Lebanon – were not very concerned with the plight of the **stateless** Palestinians. Their leaders said the right things but did nothing.

As we have seen (page 22), from the early 1950s the Palestinians had been taking things into their own hands by organizing *fedayeen* raids into Israel. In 1959 a new Palestinian organization, *Fatah* (meaning 'Victory' or 'Conquest'), was established to co-ordinate this activity. Among its leaders was a man who would play a key role in Palestinian affairs for the rest of the century, Yasser Arafat.

Independent Palestinian activity worried the Arab leaders. In an effort to control it, in 1964 Nasser helped set up the Palestine Liberation Organization (**PLO**) with a Palestine National Council (PNC) to oversee political activity, and the Palestine Liberation Army (PLA) as a military wing. Although Nasser appointed the PLO's first head and kept a close eye on the organization, the *fedayeen* were soon active again. The *fedayeen's* attacks on Israeli targets, blowing up vehicles and bombing important buildings, helped trigger yet another Arab-Israeli war in 1967.

Palestinian troops training in the **Gaza Strip**, 1966. When these regular troops failed to make any impression on the Israeli forces later in the year, the Palestinians turned to **terrorism**.

President Nasser on the Palestinian problem
President Nasser of Egypt frequently referred to the
Palestinian problem in his speeches, usually linking Israeli
[**Zionist**] action with that of 'imperialists' (empire
builders) – Britain, France and the USA. Despite all his talk
of 'sacred duty', however, he seemed more concerned
with controlling the Palestinians than helping them.

The people of Palestine, and we, are working for the
restoration of their rights in their homeland. The rights of
the people of Palestine are Arab rights above all. We feel it
is our sacred duty to regain those rights for the people of
Palestine. . . [1960]

I hear the strong call for the **liberation** of this Arab territory
of Palestine, and I would like to tell you, Brethren, that all
that we are now doing is just part of the battle for
Palestine. Once we are fully emancipated [set free] from the
shackles [chains] of **colonialism** and the intrigues of
colonialist agents, we shall take a further step forward
towards the liberation of Palestine.
   When we have brought our armed forces to full strength
and made our own armaments we will take another step
forward towards the liberation of Palestine, and when we
have manufactured jet aircraft and tanks, we will embark
upon the final stage of this liberation. . . [1960]

It is not enough to deliver speeches declaring that we
would liberate Palestine and liberate it just on paper for
political consumption. . . [1963]

The Armed Forces are getting ready for the restoration of
the rights of the Palestinian people because the Palestine
battle was a smear on the entire Arab nation. No one can
forget the shame brought by the battle of 1948. The rights
of the Palestinian people must be restored. [1963]

The Six-Day War, 1967

The trigger that fired the third Arab-Israeli war – the Six-Day War – appeared when a strongly anti-**Zionist** government came to power in Syria (1966) and allied with Egypt. Israeli fears mounted and serious armed clashes continued into 1967. In May, acting on a false Russian report that Israeli troops were gathering for an attack on Syria, Egypt's **ally**, the Egyptians moved into **Sinai** after the region's **UN** peacekeeping force (UNEF) withdrew.

On 22 May, Nasser blockaded (prevented access to) the southern Israeli port of Elat. Two weeks later (5 June), feeling sure they were about to be attacked, the Israelis launched a massive pre-emptive air attack on Egypt, Jordan and Syria, destroying most of their airforces. Without air cover, the poorly co-ordinated Arab land forces were swept aside by the better-equipped Israelis. In less than a week the Israelis had powered across Sinai to the Suez Canal, taken all the **West Bank** of the River Jordan, and captured the vital Golan Heights on the border with Syria. They also took control of all Jerusalem, a city that had previously been divided between itself and Jordan. Israel had tripled in size. Meanwhile, its dusty paths and highways streamed with Palestinian **refugees** crossing the frontiers into neighbouring Arab states.

Modern wars are won in the air: Israeli troops inspect a downed Soviet-built Egyptian Mig 17 jet fighter. After wiping out most enemy aircraft in the first few hours of the war, Israelis were assured of victory.

The Battle of Bethlehem, the birthplace of Jesus Christ, was over in a few hours, leaving Israeli forces in complete control of the town on 9 June 1967.

A Palestinian remembers the Six-Day War

Mike, now a Palestinian refugee, vividly recalls his experiences of the 1967 Six-Day War as a six-year-old boy. It is brutal memories like these, burned into countless minds, Palestinian as well as Israeli, that make settlement of the Arab-Israeli conflict so difficult.

Shortly after the June 1967 War began, the people of our village, Beit Hanina, realized with grim reality that the Israeli army would be coming here: the realization brought panic; people began to prepare to flee their homes. . . My mother decided to join our neighbours as they fled with their families to the surrounding caves in the hills overlooking our village. . .

Shortly before sunset, we took what we could carry and ran to the hills. After a long and arduous climb, we made our way to a large cave whose opening faced Jerusalem, providing a vantage point for viewing the battle raging in the distance. Already inside the cave were about seventeen people, mostly women and children . . .
I made my way to the cave's mouth and sat down to watch the 'fireworks show' lighting the night sky. Fear and anxiety could be seen on all the faces of the adults inside, but the only noise was the crying of my infant nephew and the muffled weeping of the women. . . We had left our homes and all we had behind, and now we were sharing our fate in a cave infested with snakes and scorpions.

27

Resolution 242

The Six-Day War left Israel stronger than ever, a point noted by the USA, which now regarded Israel as its principal **ally** in the region. This counterbalanced the **Soviet Union**'s links with Egypt and Syria, but made the Arab-Israeli divide deeper than ever. The war also badly damaged Nasser's prestige and undermined his idea of a single 'Arab nation'. Increasingly, the driving forces in the Middle East were individual nationalities and **militant Islam**.

The United Nations Security Council, meeting during the Six-Day War of 1967, for once spoke with a united voice in calling on both sides to cease hostilities.

After much discussion and argument, the **UN Security Council** passed the famous Resolution 242 demanding a just settlement based on the concept of 'peace for land' (see page 29). The fine words were largely ignored for 25 years. Meanwhile, Israelis and their Arab neighbours fought a limited war of **attrition** (1967–1970) and the Palestinians, frustrated by the failures of their fellow Arabs, continued their build-up of independent power.

The Security Council's solution for peace
The UN Security Council's Resolution 242 might have
been a basis for peace in the Middle East if the Council
had been united in seeing it carried through.
Unfortunately, the split between the **communist Soviet
Union** and the **democratic-capitalist** USA made
agreement to act impossible.

The Security Council makes clear its continuing worry over
the serious situation in the Middle East. It also wants to
emphasise the illegality of gaining territory by war, and the
need to work for a just and lasting peace in which every
State in the area can live in security. . .

1. The Security Council states that to meet the principles
set out in the [UN] Charter the bringing of a just and lasting
peace to the Middle East should include. . .

(i) Withdrawal of Israeli armed forces from territories
    occupied in the recent conflict;

(ii) Ending of all war, and respect for and recognition of . . .
    every State in the area and their right to live in peace
    within secure and recognised boundaries free from
    threats or acts of force;

2. The Security Council sets out the need (a) To guarantee
freedom of navigation through international waterways in
the area; (b) To achieve a just settlement of the **refugee**
problem; (c) To guarantee the territorial security and
political independence of every State in the area through
measures including the establishment of **demilitarized
zones**.

3. The Security Council requests the Secretary-General [head
of the UN] to appoint a Special representative for the Middle
East . . . who shall encourage agreement and help efforts to
achieve a peaceful settlement agreed by all sides. . .

Arab versus Arab

The Six-Day War brought 600,000 Palestinian Arabs under Israeli rule in the **West Bank**, and another 300,000 in the densely populated **Gaza Strip**, 40 kilometres (25 miles) long and 6 to 8 kilometres (4 to 5 miles) wide. Israel now contained about 3 million Israeli Jews and 1.2 million Arabs.

Many Arabs lived in poverty and were often discriminated against by the Israelis. The better-paid jobs, for instance, nearly always went to Jews. Understandably, Palestinians were attracted to the **PLO** and its organizations that acted with it. These included *Fatah* (see page 24), the Popular Front for the Liberation of Palestine (PFLP), and the Democratic Front for the Liberation of Palestine (DFLP). From 1969 the PLO chairman Yasser Arafat was generally acknowledged as leader of the Palestinian movement.

Arab summit meeting, 12 September 1970. The rare gathering of (left to right) Libya's Colonel Gadaffi, Palestinian leader Yasser Arafat, Egypt's President Nasser and King Hussein of Jordan sought to end the **civil war** within Jordan.

Driven from the West Bank by the Israelis, in 1968–69 the PLO and its fighters established themselves in Jordan, where a further 250,000 Palestinian **refugees** had fled to in 1967. Here, Arafat and his supporters came into armed conflict with the government of King Hussein. After two failed Palestinian assassination attempts on his life, in 1971 Hussein finally drove the Palestinian **militants** from his kingdom.

A British journalist interviews Yasser Arafat

Passionate about the Palestinian cause, Yasser Arafat was sorely tried by the lack of support from fellow Arabs and Israeli inflexibility. When interviewed by the British journalist Robert Fisk in 1980, his frustrations clearly got the better of him.

He was smiling, formally polite and insisted on speaking English. . . A principal theme was that of betrayal [by the Americans]. . . 'I hope that the American government . . . will recognise the legal rights of the Palestinian people which have been accepted by the **United Nations**.'

It was at around this moment that Arafat's mood began to undergo startling changes. One moment, he would be outlining with great care and with a quiet voice his relationship with King Hussein, the next almost choking with anger, shouting his condemnation of the '**terrorist** military junta' [group of unruly soldiers] that governed Israel. . .

In other wars, I said, the various armies of guerrillas, **insurgents**, rebels . . . seemed to be able to confine most of their attacks – not always but usually – to military and industrial targets. But the Palestinians often appeared to end up killing Israeli children and women.

The fist slammed onto the table.

'Babies. Only babies. Yes? Only babies and children. Do you believe them [the Israelis]? . . . another big lie.'

Would he not agree that Israeli civilians were killed?

'Rumours.'

But children had been killed in a recent Palestinian attack.

'Another big rumour!' Arafat was shouting . . . so loud . . . the needle in my recorder . . . flick[ed] again and again into the area of the dial marked red for warning.

31

Yom Kippur

In 1967 Israel had extended its territory to frontiers that were easily defended. Afterwards, Prime Minister Golda Meir refused to return the captured land in exchange for a peace agreement. She did not believe such an agreement would last. Not surprisingly, therefore, a fourth Arab-Israeli war began with surprise Arab attacks across the Suez Canal and into the Golan Heights on 6 October 1973, the Jewish festival of Yom Kippur. The new Egyptian leader, Anwar Sadat, and his counterpart in Syria, Hafez al-Asad, needed victory to increase their prestige. They also believed Israel would **negotiate** only under pressure.

At war once again: Israeli troops advancing across **Sinai** during the 1973 war with their Arab neighbours.

For a few days the Israelis seemed close to defeat. However, reinforced with massive supplies of US arms, they were soon on the offensive. On 24 October, the USA and the **Soviet Union** imposed a **cease-fire**. Even so, Israeli confidence had been shaken. For the first time the Arabs had enjoyed limited military success. They had also deployed a new weapon – the world's need for oil. When the war began, Arab oil-producing states had reduced oil **exports** by 25 per cent and cut them altogether to the USA and the Netherlands. The sudden shortages had severely disrupted the world economy.

The impact of Yom Kippur

The Yom Kippur War was a turning point in the Arab-Israeli conflict. As the author, Stewart Ross, recalls, military success and the oil **embargo** suddenly made many in the **West** view the Arabs in a new light.

I was in Riyadh [the capital of Saudi Arabia] when the war began. The local TV showed the usual **propaganda** material about the Arabs winning great victories and the enemy being either cowards or cruel beasts, but this time there was something different. There was a new confidence in the air. The Arabs had actually driven the enemy back, and there were pictures of this on the TV. I speak of 'the enemy', by the way, because the terms 'Israel' and 'Israeli' were banned. On every imported map, even in a newspaper, the name 'Israel' was scribbled out with black felt pen.

I didn't realize the impact of the oil embargo when I was in Saudi Arabia. However, when I returned home to Britain for a holiday that winter, it was like a nightmare sci-fi movie: lower speed limits for drivers, a three-day working week, power cuts, freezing houses, unemployment rising, **inflation**. I know it wasn't all due to the cut in Arab oil, but that had a huge impact. People now knew where Saudi Arabia was, which they didn't when I first went there. What's more, they took the Arabs seriously. They were people who mattered – they could hurt us.

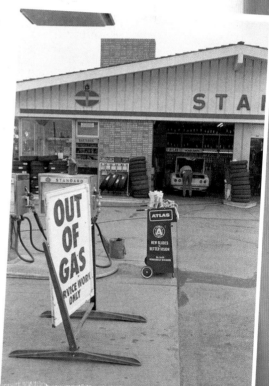

Oil war: the Arab oil embargo imposed on the USA in 1973 caused immense dislocation and anger. This sign in Denver, Colorado, was mirrored right across the country.

33

The conflict spreads

After the ejection of the **PLO** and its *fedayeen* fighters from Jordan in 1971 and the Yom Kippur War of 1973, the focus of the Arab-Israeli conflict divided. It was drawn partly towards lengthy peace talks between Israel and Egypt (see page 36), and partly towards Lebanon. Most Arab countries, particularly Lebanon, contained a proportion of Christians. The Lebanese constitution had been carefully designed to enable the country's different religious communities to live and work together. In 1975 this constitution collapsed and a long and bitter **civil war** between Christians and Muslims began. Tragically, both Israel and the Palestinians became involved.

On being forced from Jordan, Palestinian **militants** had made Lebanon their base and organized frequent raids over its southern border into Israel. Not surprisingly, these Palestinians were drawn into the civil war on the side of the Lebanese Muslims. The Israelis backed the Christians. Over the next three years, before a **UN**-arranged **cease-fire**, Syrian and Israeli forces moved into Lebanon and there were horrifying civilian casualties.

A once thriving city: the devastation of Beirut, capital of Lebanon, caused by a Christian-Muslim civil war and foreign intervention.

A conversation with Sammi Habib

Sammi Habib, a middle-class Christian Lebanese businessman, was intensely proud of his country. The civil war that broke out in 1975 left him disillusioned, bitter and bankrupt.

You remember Lebanon, don't you? You came there with me, remember, and we had a good time? It was a great place. Fantastic! The best place in all the Middle East, where **East** and **West** met. Well, all that's gone. You've seen it on TV, but it's worse than that. You can't imagine what it's like now.

Street fighting in Beirut, 1975. The immensely complicated mix of national, religious and political factors made the conflict very difficult to resolve.

There is no trust – I can do business with Christians only, and they want more money, a sort of war tax to pay for the fighting. I haven't anything left.

Some of my family have been killed. My aunt – my mother's sister, the one who lived in Beirut – she died when her house was hit by a shell. We could not find the pieces of her body. My uncle had a heart attack afterwards and he died. Curse them!

Can you imagine guns firing in those lovely streets? It's evil, I really believe that. And, I tell you, I don't think it was our fault. We would have been OK, just getting on fine, without the Israelis and the Palestinians. They spoil everything. They are like a disease that spreads out and out. Now it has come to my country and ruined it. I can't believe it. It would have been fine without those **refugees** and their camps and their fighters.

Camp David

From the outset of the Arab-Israeli conflict it was clear that Egypt and Jordan put their own interests before those of the Palestinians. Jordan clearly showed this when it occupied the **West Bank** in 1948. It was Egypt, however, that made the boldest move: in 1978 President Sadat broke step with the rest of the Arab world and made a separate peace agreement with Israel.

Sadat's visit to Israel in 1977 had been the first ever official contact of an Arab state with Israel. It was followed by intense **negotiations**, presided over by US President Jimmy Carter, that ended with agreement at Camp David, the presidential country retreat. Israel handed back **Sinai**, and both countries resumed full **diplomatic** and economic relations. Three years later Sadat was **assassinated** by an **Islamic** extremist.

The Palestinians had featured in the Israeli-Egyptian agreement, although they were not invited to the talks. The Israeli **hard-line** prime minister, Menachem Begin, had accepted some self-administration for Palestinians in the West Bank and **Gaza Strip**, but the idea had fizzled out in later negotiation.

A rare glimmer of hope. President Anwar Sadat of Egypt, US President Jimmy Carter and Israeli Prime Minister Menachem Begin at the signing of the historical peace accord in Washington DC on 26 March 1979.

An Arab president addresses the Israeli parliament

On 20 November 1977, the Egyptian President Anwar Sadat spoke before the Israeli parliament. This remarkable gesture by a very brave man greatly helped break down Arab-Israeli hatred and led to lasting peace between Israel and Egypt.

In the name of God. . . I come to you today on solid ground to shape a new life and to establish peace. We all love this land, the land of God, we all, Muslims, Christians and Jews, all worship God. . .

We all still bear the consequences of four fierce wars waged within 30 years. All this at the time when the families of the 1973 October war are still mourning under the cruel pain of bereavement of father, son, husband and brother.

. . . Any life that is lost in war is a human life . . . Arab or Israeli. A wife who becomes a widow is a human being entitled to a happy family life, whether she be an Arab or an Israeli.

Paying the price: the funeral of Egypt's peace-making president Anwar Sadat in 1981. He had been assassinated by extremist anti-Israeli terrorists.

Innocent children who are deprived of the care and compassion of their parents are ours. . . For the sake of them all, for the sake of the lives of all our sons and brothers . . . for the generations to come, for a smile on the face of every child born in our land, for all that I have taken my decision to come to you . . . to deliver my address.

Mounting violence

As far as the Palestinians were concerned, the Camp David agreement solved nothing. Elsewhere, things were looking up for the **PLO**. By 1980 over 80 countries had recognized it as a legitimate organization, thereby admitting that Palestine had a right to exist. This number did not include the USA, however, which would not accept the PLO while it refused either to recognize Israel or to renounce **terrorism**.

The PLO received international support and money, especially from Saudi Arabia and Libya. The Saudis, although friendly with the **West**, were eager to keep in with their fellow Arabs. Libya was hostile to Israel because of its alliance with the US. Thus funded, the PLO continued its cross-border attacks on Israel from Lebanon. The conflict spread, too, with an attempted **assassination** of Israel's **ambassador** to Britain.

Ready to die for their cause, a group of Muslim Hezbollah guerrillas in a display of solidarity outside a Palestinian refugee camp, 28 January 1987.

To put an end to Palestinian raids, in 1982 Israeli forces invaded Lebanon. Sweeping away all resistance, their armoured vehicles crushed the PLO and their Syrian **allies**, and forced Arafat and his accomplices (helpers) from the country. Thousands were killed. Arafat relocated himself in Tunisia and, in 1985, some members of his government moved to Saddam Hussein's Iraq. Meanwhile, anti-Israeli and often anti-Western terrorism, in the form of new groups such *Hezbollah* (the Party of God, 1982), was becoming increasingly **Islamic**. In other words, stronger links were being made between the Palestinian cause and fanatical Islam – Muslim extremists were saying it was a 'religious duty' to wipe out Israel.

The findings of an official enquiry

On 16 September 1982 occurred one of the greatest horrors of the Arab-Israeli conflict, when a force of Israeli-backed Lebanese Christians, the **Phalange**, pursued their enemies into the Sabra and Shatilla Palestinian **refugee** camps and slaughtered between 800 and 2000 civilians. This is an excerpt from the official Israeli **commission** of inquiry into the **massacres**.

On Thursday, 17 September 1982, at approximately 6:00 p.m., members of the Phalangists entered the Shatilla camp . . . [Their] movements within the camps were not visible. . . The [Israeli] Divisional Intelligence Officer tried to follow their movements using binoculars which he shifted from place to place, but was unable to see their movements or their actions...

At approximately 8:00 p.m . . . an [Israeli] Intelligence officer... received a report according to which the Phalangists' liaison officer had heard via radio from one of the Phalangists inside the camps that he was holding 45 people. That person asked what he should do with the people, and the liaison officer's reply was "Do the will of God," or words to that effect. . .

At about the same time or slightly earlier, at approximately 7:00 p.m., Lieutenant Elul [an Israeli soldier] . . . overheard another conversation that took place over the Phalangists' transmitter. . . He heard a Phalangist officer from the force that had entered the camps tell Elie Hobeika [Phalange officer] . . . that there were 50 women and children, and what should he do. Elie Hobeika's reply over the radio was: 'This is the last time you're going to ask me a question like that, you know exactly what to do,' and then raucous laughter broke out among the Phalangist personnel on the roof. Lieutenant Elul understood that what was involved was the murder of the women and children.

Intifada

At the extreme **right** of Israeli opinion were the **Zionists** who believed all Israel's territory was God-given. They called for more Jewish settlements on the **West Bank** which Israel had captured in 1967. Directly opposite the Israeli Zionists were non-religious **left**-wingers. Feeling guilty about their country's aggression, they sought an early and generous settlement with the Palestinians. As violence mounted during the 1980s, both sides became more set in their positions.

Isolated in Tunisia, Yasser Arafat changed tactics. From 1982 onwards, violence having failed, he began to seek a **diplomatic** settlement to the Palestinian problem based on his supporters stopping violence in return for the Palestinians having their own state. His authority and approach were increasingly challenged by **Hamas**. This was another anti-Israeli group of **Islamic** extremists.

Unexpectedly, in December 1987 the Palestinian situation changed when the Palestinians of the West Bank and **Gaza Strip** began spontaneous resistance known as the *Intifada*. Men, women and children made life as difficult as possible for the Israelis. They went on

strike, refused to have any form of business or contact, refused to co-operate in everyday government, and organized violent, stone-throwing demonstrations. The Israeli government reacted with violence. Within a year 300 Palestinians had been killed, 11,500 wounded (the majority under the age of fifteen), and thousands imprisoned. The watching world was not impressed.

A defiant Palestinian woman leads an anti-Israeli protest before the banned Palestinian flag.

In the name of God, the merciful, the compassionate. Call, call,
call. No voice can rise above the voice of the uprising; no voice
can rise above the voice of the Palestinian people, the people of
the PLO.

O masses of our great people: Your triumphant uprising is now
beginning its sixth month, defying the wounds; embracing the
Palestinian sky through **martyrdom** and victory, challenging all
kinds of oppression, tyranny, and killing which our enemy is
pursuing; opening the door to our triumphant revolution
[complete change] and the originator of our struggle, the PLO;
exposing our enemies' ugly faces before the whole world; foiling
all the conspiratorial projects against our steadfast people;
strengthening our people's unity around the PLO, the sole
legitimate representative; and protecting our independent
decision-making. There will be no trusteeship or alternative
except Palestine, the alternative which is baptised with the blood
of our righteous martyrs. . .

O masses of our struggling people, the PLO – the Unified
National Leadership – calls on all segments of our people to
mark the following days with sweeping mass anger . . . and
implementing the following **militant** activities:

First, dedicating 28 and 29 May to massive marches and
rallies. . .

Second, dedicating 30 May to an all-out strike. . .

Third, dedicating 1 June – International Children's Day – to
children's demonstrations raising Palestinian slogans and flags.

PLO recognition and isolation

In November and December 1988, at the height of the *Intifada*, Yasser Arafat made a dramatic move: he declared Palestine an independent state (much as David Ben Gurion had done with Israel in 1948), and then, despite all he had said to the contrary, he recognized the existence of Israel and rejected all forms of **terrorism**. On these announcements, the USA said it was prepared to talk with the **PLO**. Israel's **conservative** leader, Yitzhak Shamir, however, still refused.

Arafat's initiative was undone by his **ally**, Iraqi leader Saddam Hussein, who invaded Kuwait in August 1990. The aggression was universally condemned, except by the Palestinians, Libya, Sudan, Jordan and Yemen. The next year a US-led **coalition**, operating out of Saudi Arabia, **liberated** Kuwait and destroyed most of Iraq's armed forces. Arab funds for the PLO dried up. Finding themselves bankrupt and increasingly isolated, the Palestinians were unable to maintain their level of armed resistance, and **negotiation** became crucial (see page 44).

An Iraqi Scud missile falls on the Israeli city of Tel Aviv during the 1991 Gulf War. The Israelis, worried that the conflict might escalate, did not respond.

The Eastern bloc [group of allied states], led by the USSR,
supported the Arabs basic rights, including their rights in the
Arab-**Zionist** conflict. . . And suddenly, the situation changed in a
dramatic way. The USSR turned to tackle its domestic problems
. . . [and] it has become clear to everyone that the United States
has emerged in a superior position. . .

[Therefore] the Arabs must take into account that there is a real
possibility that Israel might embark on new stupidities . . . as a
result of direct or tacit [unspoken] US encouragement. On the
other hand, the Arabs have a plus, and that is Arab solidarity. . .

Brothers, the weakness of a big body lies in its bulkiness. All
strong men have their Achilles heel [weak point]. Therefore,
irrespective of our known stand on terror and terrorists, we saw
that the United States as a superpower departed Lebanon
immediately [1983] when some Marines [part of a peace-keeping
force] were killed. They were, the very men who are considered to
be the most prominent symbol of its arrogance . . . Israel, once
dubbed the invincible country, has been defeated by some of the
Arabs. The resistance put up by Palestinians and Lebanese militia
against Israeli invasion forces in 1982, and before that the heroic
crossing of the Suez canal in 1973, have had a more telling
psychological and actual impact than all Arab threats.

Signs of hope, 1991–96

For Jews and Arabs life in Israel during the *Intifada* remained difficult and dangerous. It was a painful round of security checks, delays and disruptions. Every now and again came sudden, bloody murders. When these occurred, the Israeli security forces issued harsh and often inaccurate punishment for every hurt.

Elsewhere, however, the ending of the **Cold War** was bringing benefits. The USA, less reliant on Israel as its Middle East **ally**, could pressure it to **negotiate** by threatening to cut aid. In 1991, backed by the US, talks opened in Madrid, Spain, between Israel and various Arab states. These were followed by the election of an Israeli **Labour** government willing to negotiate in 1992. This produced a breakthrough in Oslo, Norway, in 1993.

Another step towards peace? US President Bill Clinton watches over the historic handshake between Israeli Prime Minister Yitzhak Rabin (left) and **PLO** Chairman Yasser Arafat, on 13 September 1993.

Prime Minister Yitzhak Rabin and Yasser Arafat agreed in the Oslo Accords [agreements] that administration of **Gaza** and the **West Bank** would be gradually handed over to elected officials of a Palestinian Authority. Here, at last, was a major breakthrough.

Despite the efforts of extremists on both sides to derail the agreement, in 1994 Israeli forces left the Gaza Strip and part of the West Bank, and their government made a formal peace with Jordan. Tragically, though, on 4 November 1995 an Israeli extremist shot Rabin dead for supposedly betraying the Jewish people.

A description of the killer of Prime Minister Rabin

The complexity of the Arab-Israeli problem is illustrated by this article in *The Times* of London about the killer of Yitzhak Rabin. The young man was clearly as fanatical about his cause as any **Hamas** extremist was about theirs.

THE TIMES

6 November 1995

The gunman, a Jewish law student, yesterday made a detailed confession to Israeli police in which he said he had shot Yitzhak Rabin and was happy he had died. Mr Amir, 25, said he had twice before attempted to be close enough to **assassinate** the Prime Minister...

In another . . . interview earlier this year, the assassin said the Jews would always control the West Bank despite Israel's attempts to concede 'the most holy land' for peace... Standing in an illegal new Jewish settlement . . . in the upper West Bank, Mr Amir said: 'This is the most holy land. Two thousand years ago most of the population of Israel was here.'

. . . Asked about the Arab villages near by, planted with orchards of apple and almond trees, he [said] . . . 'Because they work the land, it does not mean it belongs to the Arabs.'

. . . [He] lived and worked amid senior representatives of the Yesha Council, the umbrella organisation [largest organization] for Jewish settlers, and of Likud Youth. The encampment was filled with placards and banners stating 'The Land of Israel is in Danger'. After the shooting, Mr Amir told Israeli police interrogators that he had 'received instructions from God to kill Rabin' and had acted alone.

The Jewish extremist Yigal Amir (centre) while on trial for the assassination of Yitzhak Rabin, 1996.

Terror and counter-terror

Following the murder of Prime Minister Rabin in 1995, the peace process stumbled towards collapse. There were talks and even agreements, but always the efforts of the USA, the **PLO**, and Israeli governments of the **left** and **right** failed in the face of **militant** Israeli and Palestinian opposition. Tired of all the talk and empty promises, in autumn 2000 the Palestinians launched a second *Intifada*.

Palestinian militants, organized by the **terrorist** groups **Hamas** and **Islamic Jihad**, turned to suicide bombings. Young people, told they would become **martyrs**, tied explosives around their bodies and detonated them in crowded places popular with Israelis, like shopping malls or night-clubs and on packed buses. The death, mutilation and destruction are difficult to imagine.

Each time this happened, the Israelis responded by making arrests, flattening the houses or districts from which they believed the bombers to have come, and killing suspected terrorists and their sympathizers. And each attack and **reprisal** brought new suffering and grief, feeding the never ending cycle of hatred and revenge.

Violence as part of everyday life: a heavily-armed Israeli patrol in Jerusalem, 2000.

Orla Guerin reports from Jerusalem for the BBC
The cycle of violence is well captured in this report of a
suicide bombing in Jerusalem on 3 December 2001. TV
reporter Orla Guerin describes the wretchedness of a
particular Israeli family.

Moshe was one of ten teenagers killed on Saturday night in two
suicide bomb attacks at a pedestrian mall in Jerusalem. His
younger brother, Adam, says Moshe survived the first blast, but
his friend was wounded and as he rushed to help, he ran straight
into the path of the second suicide bomber. . .

'He wasn't even 20. He
didn't have a chance to live,'
[his mother] said. 'These
awful murderers cut off his
life. Our whole country is
soaked in blood.'

To Israelis it seems that way.

. . . The newspapers are full
of pictures of the carnage
and the stories of those
who died, like the two 15-
year-olds who had been
friends since birth and died side-by-side.
One 19-year-old was killed out on a date
with a new girlfriend.

The politics of terror: 16 Israelis
died and more than 100 were
wounded when this Israeli bus
was blown apart by a Hamas
suicide bomber on 11 June 2003.

In their grief Israelis are calling for tough
action. . . They want Yasser Arafat to be hit hard. . .

Video footage of one of the suicide bombers leaves no doubt as
to what Israel is facing. The young militant poses proudly for the
camera before issuing a chilling statement – the attacks will not
stop until Israel ends its occupation of the **West Bank** and **Gaza**.
Those areas are now under a total Israeli closure . . . [and]
innocent civilians [are] once again paying the price for what the
extremists have done. Israeli helicopter gunships have now
launched air strikes on Palestinian targets in the Gaza Strip.

The road map

The **terrorist** attacks on New York and Washington of 11 September 2001 brought the USA and Israel closer together. US thinking ran that now, both countries were fighting **fundamentalist** Muslim terror. The US government believed that settlement of the Palestinian question would help its anti-terror campaign by removing a major source of Muslim outrage.

In Israel, however, the **hard-line** government of Ariel Sharon (in power since February 2001) was unwilling to compromise – to look for a middle way. On occasion Israeli forces reoccupied much of the **West Bank**, raided the **Gaza Strip** and confined Arafat to a single battered building. Still the riots and bombings went on.

In May 2003, after successfully toppling Saddam Hussein, the USA gave its support to yet another plan. This was a '**road map** to peace', sponsored by the **UN**, the USA, the EU and Russia. Part of the plan was to bypass Arafat and talk directly with the Palestinian prime minister, Mahmoud Abbas. Like so many other schemes, however, the road map soon ran into difficulties. By the end of 2003 the hopes and fears of millions yet again rested in the balance.

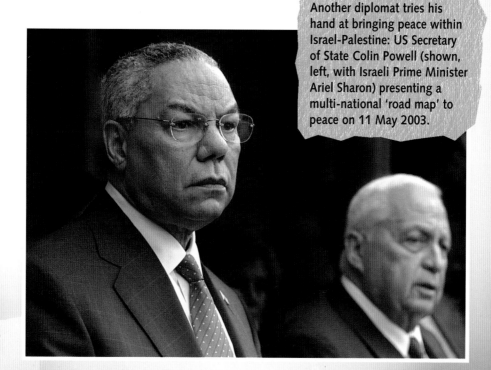

Another diplomat tries his hand at bringing peace within Israel-Palestine: US Secretary of State Colin Powell (shown, left, with Israeli Prime Minister Ariel Sharon) presenting a multi-national 'road map' to peace on 11 May 2003.

I am sick. Sick and tired. Literally, physically and politically. I am
in bed. . . I could not handle it anymore. . .

The week before, I was preoccupied with attacks on medical
personnel. On 4 March 2002, Israeli occupation troops opened
fire on an ambulance, killing 58-year-old Dr Khalil Suleiman, head of
the Palestinian Red Crescent Society Emergency Medical Service in
Jenin in the West Bank.

Four paramedics and a driver who were travelling in the ambulance
were injured. An injured girl was being transported in the ambulance
at the time. Four days later Dr Ahmad Nu'man Sabih al-Khoudari,
the director of the small Yamama Hospital in al-Khadr, was shot
dead as he drove to the al-Dheisheh **refugee** camp, on the
fringes of Bethlehem. The doctor had received assurances from
an Israeli official that his security would be respected, however,
passing a checkpoint [a place where papers are checked] he was
shot and killed by heavy Israeli fire. Since 4 March a total of five
health personnel have been killed and several others injured. . .

The last thing my eyes had seen were the original pictures of [the
death of] Mahmoud Salah [a Palestinian who had recently died in
the violence]. It choked me. I could not breathe anymore. . . I
collapsed. I was exhausted, but could not sleep. Apache helicopters,
occasional shooting and other noises kept me from sleeping.

What have we learnt?

The Arab-Israeli conflict has changed a great deal since the outbreak of war in 1948. Perhaps the most remarkable development has been the 55-year growth of the state of Israel, both in terms of territory and as a military, **economic** and political force in the region. Although Israel signed peace **treaties** with Egypt and Jordan, the core issues surrounding the conflicts of interest between Israelis and Palestinians still remain. These include the potential creation of a Palestinian state, the status of Jerusalem, the disputed Israeli settlements and the plight of Palestinian **refugees**. The cycle of violence and bloodshed is likely to continue until these issues are resolved.

So where does the conflict go from here? There are three possible routes. First, some sort of agreement may be reached for the creation of a Palestinian state alongside Israel. Second, there are those who urge Palestinians and Israelis to combine into a single state based on balance and toleration. Finally, the conflict may simply drag on as it has done for the last half century, **destabilizing** the region and bringing pain and misery to untold millions.

What can be done: downtown Ramallah, a **PLO**-governed **West Bank** city whose thriving economy was later wrecked by the resurgence of violence during the early years of the 21st century.

President Clinton on the Arab-Israeli conflict

US President Bill Clinton, like all his immediate White House predecessors, spent much time and effort trying to resolve the Palestinian question. On leaving office, he made the following observations on the problem.

The Arab-Israeli conflict is not just a morality play between good and evil. It is a conflict with a complex history, whose resolution requires balancing the needs of both sides. . . The only path to a just and durable resolution is through **negotiation** . . . based on . . . these parameters [requirements].

First, I think there can be no genuine resolution . . . without a sovereign [independent], viable, Palestinian state. . .

Second, a solution will have to be found for the Palestinian **refugees** who have suffered a great deal. . .

Third, there will be no peace, and no peace agreement, unless the Israeli people have lasting security guarantees. . .

Fourth, I come to the issue of Jerusalem, perhaps the most emotional and sensitive of all. It is a historic, cultural and political centre for both Israelis and Palestinians, a unique city. . .

Fifth and, finally, any agreement will have to mark the decision to end the conflict. . .

So I say to the Palestinians. . . and to the Israelis. . . listen, if you guys ever got together, ten years from now we would all wonder what the heck happened for 30 years before.

And the centre of energy and creativity and economic power and political influences in the entire region would be with the Israelis and the Palestinians because of their gifts. It could happen. But somebody has got to take the long leap, and there have to be somebodies on both sides. . .

Timeline

1914–18 World War I; Britain fights alongside Arabs against the Turks.
1915 With British support, Arabs begin a **revolt** against the Turks.
1918 British forces occupy Palestine.
1920–48 The **Ottoman** Province of Palestine is divided into Palestine and **Transjordan**, both British **mandates**.
1939–45 World War II.
1939 Britain imposes strict limits on Jewish **immigration** into Palestine.
1942–45 The **Holocaust**: **Nazi massacre** of some 6 million European Jews.
1945 The **Arab League** is formed.
1946 Transjordan becomes independent. Serious conflict in Palestine: Arabs versus Jews versus British.
1947 **UN General Assembly** votes to **partition** Palestine with the creation of the Jewish state of Israel.
1948 British leave Palestine. State of Israel proclaimed (14 May). Arab states declare war on Israel (15 May). War lasts to 1949, Israel expanding while Jordan absorbs the **West Bank** and Egypt the **Sinai** Peninsula. Huge numbers of Palestinian Arabs made homeless.
1967 Six-Day War (5–10 June) between Israel and Arabs. Israel occupies West Bank and **Gaza Strip**.
1967–70 Israeli-Egyptian War of **attrition**.
1971 **PLO** driven out of Jordan.
1973 October (or Yom Kippur) War: Arabs regain some prestige. Severe cuts in Arab oil **exports** cause worldwide economic downturn.
1975 Fifteen-year **civil war** breaks out in Lebanon.
1976 Syrian troops enter Lebanon.
1978 Israeli troops enter Lebanon to attack PLO. Camp David Peace Agreement between Egypt and Israel (signed 1979).
1980–88 Iran-Iraq War.
1981 Israel annexes Golan Heights on border with Syria.
1982 Israel invades Lebanon again. Multinational peacekeeping force moves into Lebanon. PLO driven from Lebanon. Massacre of Palestinians by the **Phalange** in Lebanese Sabra and Shatilla **refugee** camps.
1987 *Intifada* begins (continues until 1993).
1988 PLO declares the state of Palestine. Yasser Arafat renounces violence.
1990 Iraq invades Kuwait, supported by PLO.
1991 Gulf War, Iraqis driven from Kuwait. Israel refuses to be drawn into the conflict. Middle East Peace talks begin in Madrid.
1993 The PLO and Israel agree the Declaration of Principles in Oslo.
1994 A series of PLO-Israeli agreements take place. Israeli troops leave Gaza and some of West Bank. Jordan and Israel make peace.
2000 Israel makes peace with Lebanon. Second *Intifada* begins.
2001 **Hard-line** Ariel Sharon becomes Israeli prime minister. Violence mounts on both sides. 11 September **terrorist** attack on New York and Washington.
2002 Israel reoccupies most of West Bank. US, Russia, UN and EU suggest a 'road map' for peace.
2003 US-led **coalition** invades Iraq and ousts Saddam Hussein. Ongoing terrorism and **reprisals** as efforts are made to get agreement on the 'road map' to peace.

Find out more

Books & websites

Causes and Consequences of the Arab-Israeli Conflict, Stewart
Ross (Evans, 1995)
Conflict in the Middle East, John King (Wayland, 1993)
*The Fateful Triangle: The United States, Israel and the
Palestinians*, Noam Chomsky (Pluto Press, 2003)
Troubled World: The Arab-Israeli Conflict, Ivan Minnis
(Heinemann Library, 2001)

There are many websites relating to this topic, most giving
either the Israeli or Arab point of view. Somewhere in the
middle are:

http://www.cbc.ca/news/indepth/mideast_struggle
http://news.bbc.co.uk/1/hi/world/middle_east/2938444.stm
http://www.mtholyoke.edu/acad/intrel/me.htm

List of primary sources

The author and publisher gratefully acknowledge the following publications and websites from
which written sources in the book are drawn. In some cases the wording or sentence structure has
been simplified to make the material more appropriate for a school readership.
p.9 Theodor Herzl: 'The Jewish State', 1896, cited in *The Israel-Arab Reader*, Walter Laquer and
Barry Rubin (Penguin, revised edition, 2001)
p.11 Both quotes cited in *Arab-Israeli Conflict and Conciliation: A Documentary History*, Bernard
Reich (ed) (Praeger, 1995)
p.13 The Royal Commission's report, cited in: *The Israel-Arab Reader*, Walter Laquer and Barry
Rubin (Penguin, revised edition, 2001)
p.15 Cited on http://www.ushmm.org/museum/exhibit/online/phistories
p.17 UN General Assembly's partition resolution, cited in *The Israel-Arab Reader*, Walter Laquer
and Barry Rubin (Penguin, revised edition, 2001)
p.19 Alfred M. Lilienthal, *Readers Digest*, New York, September 1949
p.21 Personal interview with the author Stewart Ross in 1973
p.23 The Sèvres Protocol, 1956, cited in *The Arab-Israeli Conflict*, Kirsten E Schulze (Pearson, 1999)
p.25 President Nasser, cited in *The Israel-Arab Reader*, Walter Laquer and Barry Rubin (Penguin,
revised edition, 2001)
p.27 From Palestine Monitor on:
http://www.palestinemonitor.org/Feature/Nakba_and_Memories.htm
p.29 UN Security Council's Resolution 242, cited, inter alia in *The Arab-Israeli Conflict*, Kirsten E
Schulze (Pearson, 1999)
p.31 *Pity the Nation: Lebanon at War* (André Deutsch, 1990)
p. 33 Author's personal recollection
p.35 From a conversation with the author, 1976
p.37 Cited on http://www.ibiblio.org/sullivan/docs/Knesset-speech.html
p.39 From the official Israeli commission of inquiry into the massacres, cited on
http://www.mfa.gov.il/mfa/go.asp?MFAH0ign0
p.41 PLO pamphlet, cited in *The Israel-Arab Reader*, Walter Laquer and Barry Rubin (Penguin,
revised edition, 2001)
p.43 Speech by Saddam Hussein, cited in *Anti-American Terrorism in the Middle East: A
Documentary Reader*, Barry Rubin & Judith Colp Rubin (eds) (Oxford, 2002)
p.45 Ross Dunn and Tom Rhodes in *The Times*, 6 November 1995
p.47 A BBC report on http://news.bbc.co.uk/1/hi/world/middle_east
p.49 Report from Arjan El Fassed cited on http://electronic*intifada*.net/v2/article647.shtml
p.51 Bill Clinton's speech in New York, 2001, cited in *The Israel-Arab Reader*, Walter Laquer and
Barry Rubin (Penguin, revised edition, 2001)

Glossary

ally partner, usually in war

ambassador official representative of one country in another

Arab League co-operation of Arab states set up in 1945

assassinate murder for political reasons

attrition gradual wearing down of the enemy

capitalist political and economic system that believes in individuals and businesses being free to buy and sell as they wish without government interference or control

cease-fire agreement to stop fighting but not necessarily to make peace

civil war war between different groups in one country

coalition group working together

Cold War period when the capitalist West, led by the USA, and the communist East, led by the Soviet Union, lived on the brink of a fighting war, 1946–89

colonialism acquisition of overseas territory by another country, and for the benefit of that country

commando soldiers who operate in secret

commission group of people officially appointed to carry out certain work or an official order for a task to be undertaken, such as an inquiry

communism political and economic system based on the idea of the state owning all property and wealth and sharing it out equally between all citizens

conservative liking traditional ways and cautious about change

demilitarized zone area where military activity is not allowed

democracy government of the people, by the people, for the people

destabilize make less stable

diplomacy official relations between nations

East (as opposed to 'West' in this book) Soviet Union and its communist allies

embargo trade ban

export sell goods from one country to another country

fedayeen Palestinian guerrillas

fundamentalist one who believes in every word of their faith, not allowing for any subtleties or double meanings

Gaza Strip narrow strip of land along the eastern shore of the Mediterranean, south of Israel, around the city of Gaza

Great Depression time when the world's economy was in a serious down-turn, 1929–39

General Assembly United Nations' parliament in which all states have a voice

Hamas Palestinian organization (official title: Islamic Resistance Movement) pledged to destroying Israel by any means

hard-line unwilling to compromise

Hezbollah Muslim fundamentalist organization pledged to the overthrow of Israel by any means

Holocaust Nazi attempt to wipe out all European Jews

immigration people leaving one country to live in another

inflation when the value of money falls and prices rise

insurgent rebel

Intifada Palestinian uprising against the Israelis

Islam Muslim religion

Islamic/Islamist relating to Islam

Islamic Jihad Muslim fundamentalist organization pledged to violence, especially suicide bombings

Judaism religion of the Jews

Labour left-wing Israeli political party

League of Nations international organization set up after World War I to keep the peace and encourage international understanding and co-operation

left (wing) describes groups that want a fairer or more equal society

liberate set free

mandate territory governed by another on behalf of the League of Nations

martyr one who dies for their religious faith

massacre mass killing

militant aggressive, unwilling to compromise

nationalism vigorous enthusiasm for one's country

Nazi German National Socialist Party of Adolf Hitler

negotiate discuss in order to reach an agreement

Ottoman relating to the old Turkish Empire

partition divide up

Phalange Lebanese Christian party

pilgrim one who travels to a special religious site

PLO Palestine Liberation Organization, the main organization representing the Palestinians since 1964

primary source direct evidence about historical events

propaganda information or opinion slanted to favour a particular point of view

refugee one who flees from danger or repression

reprisal violent action taken as a response to a previous action

retaliate take action in response to a previous action

revolt rebellion

right (wing) describes parties and individuals that favour established forms of society, authority and order

road map Middle East peace plan sponsored by the USA, United Nations, the EU and Russia

secondary source historical account written some time after the events described have taken place

Security Council decision-making body of the United Nations

Sinai peninsular to the east of the Suez Canal

Soviet Union communist empire based on Russia, 1922–91

stateless not belonging to a country, without a passport

superpower major world power

terrorism violent action against ordinary people in an attempt to gain certain political goals

Transjordan previous name of the kingdom of Jordan

treaty formal agreement between countries

United Nations (UN) International organization set up in 1945 to help encourage world peace, understanding and co-operation

USSR Soviet Union (Union of Socialist Soviet Republics)

West Democratic-capitalist states of North America, Europe and Australia and New Zealand

West Bank area between the Israeli border and the River Jordan

Zionism movement formed to create and hold a Jewish homeland in Palestine

Index

Abdullah of Transjordan, King 16
al-Asa, Hafez 32
Allenby, General Edmund 12
Arab-Israeli conflict, roots of 4-5, 8
Arab-Israeli War 1948-49 18, 21, 22
Arab-Israeli War (1967) 24
Arab League 16
Arab Revolt of 1936, 12, 13
Arafat, Yasser 7, 24, 30, 31, 38, 40, 42, 44, 48

Balfour, Arthur J 10-11
Begin, Prime Minister Menachim 36
Beirut 34-35
Ben Gurion, Prime Minister David 18, 22
Britain 10-11, 12-13, 14, 16, 17, 20, 22-23, 32

Camp David agreement 36, 38
Carter, President Jimmy 36
Clinton, President Bill 51
Cold War 5, 20, 44

Democratic Front for the Liberation of
    Palestine (DFLP) 30

Egypt 18, 22-23, 24, 26, 28, 32, 36, 50
European Union (EU) 48

Fatah 24, 30
fedayeen, the 22, 24, 34
France 20, 22-23

Gaza Strip, 18, 20, 30, 36, 40, 44, 47, 48
Germany 14
Golan Heights 5, 26, 32
Gulf War (1991) 42

Hamas 40, 41, 46
Hezbolla 38
Holocaust, the 14-15, 16
Hussein I of Jordan, King 20, 30
Hussein, Saddam 38, 42-43, 48

Intifada 7, 40-41, 42, 44, 46
Iraq 18, 38, 42-43
Islamic Jihad 46
Israel, creation of 18-19
Israel, extension of 18, 26, 30, 32

Jerusalem 8, 16-17, 26
Jewish immigration to Palestine 12, 14
Jews, dispersal of 8
Jews, persecution of 8-9, 14-15, 16
Jordan 18, 20, 24, 26, 30, 34, 36, 50

Kuwait 42

League of Nations 12
Lebanon 4, 18, 20, 24, 34-35, 38, 39, 43
Libya 38

McMahon, Sir Henry 10-11
Meir, Prime Minister Golda 32
Munich Olympic Games 7

Nasser, Prime Minister Gamal Abdul 22, 23,
    24, 25, 26, 28
nationalism 4, 9, 10, 19
Nazi party 14, 15

oil embargo 32-33
Oslo Accords 44

Palestine 8, 10, 11, 12, 13, 14, 16, 17, 18
Palestine Liberation Army (PLA) 24
Palestine Liberation Organization (PLO) 24,
    30, 34, 38, 41, 42
Palestine National Council (PNC) 24
Palestine, partition of 12, 16-17
Palestinian Arab refugees 18, 20-21, 26, 27,
    39, 50
Phalange 39
Popular Front for the Liberation of Palestine
    (PFLP) 30

Rabin, Prime Minister Yitzhak 44-45, 46
Resolution 242 28-29
'road map to peace' 48

Sabra and Shatilla refugee camps, 39
Sadat, President Anwar 32, 36-37
Saudi Arabia 21, 32, 38, 42
Sèvres agreement 23
Shamir, Prime Minister Yitzhak 42
Sharif Hussein 10-11
Sharon, Ariel 7, 48
Sinai 26, 36
Six-Day War 6, 26-27, 28, 30
Soviet Union 15, 20, 22, 28, 29, 39
Suez canal 22-23, 26, 32
suicide bombers 5, 7, 46-47
Syria 18, 24, 26, 28, 32

terrorism 5, 7, 24, 42, 43, 48
Transjordan (see Jordan)
Turkey 8, 10, 12

United Nations 16, 18, 22, 26, 28-29, 31, 34, 48
United States of America 5, 14, 16, 20, 22, 29,
    32, 38, 42, 43, 44, 48
USSR (see Soviet Union)

Weizmann, President Chaim 18
West Bank 18, 20, 22, 26, 30, 36, 40, 44, 47, 48
World War I 10, 12, 13
World War II 14

Yom Kippur War 32-33, 34

Zionists 10-11, 16, 19, 40

Titles in the *Witness to History* series include:

Hardback   0 431 17074-6

Hardback   0 431 17055-X

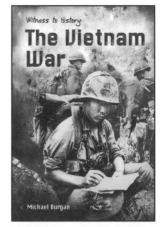

Hardback   0 431 17054-1

Hardback   0 431 17057-6

Hardback   0 431 17056-8

Hardback   0 431 17064-9

Hardback   0 431 17067-3

Hardback   0 431 17066-5

Find out about the other titles in this series on our website www.heinemann.co.uk/library